PREFACE

Thank you for purchasing this book, my Friend!

I wrote this book to share more information on how to scale your Amazon selling business and earn higher profits.

This book is something special because I'm co-writing this book with my best friend, Dan Johnson. He wrote several books about selling on Amazon FBA. He authored the best-selling e-book, **Amazon FBA: Complete Guide**.

And because Amazon sellers are important to us, Dan will be sharing his best tips and secrets on how to be a successful Amazon seller.

I believe that success needs to be sustainable and it will require mastery of the basics to grow an Amazon FBA business. I will share the best practices in Amazon FBA which makes your business efficient and eventually leads to a tremendous growth of your selling business.

Topics like inventory management, product sourcing, and repricing will be tackled in this book. I'm very excited to share with you the process on how to get more profits with Amazon FBA.

I want this book to fill up the knowledge gap on Amazon sellers who needs reliable information. Everything in this book will help you to execute the most recommended strategy to earn more in Amazon FBA selling.

Have a wonderful journey with Amazon FBA!

David Goldenberg

FOREWORD

Hi, Friend! It's a great experience to co-write this book with my best buddy, David Goldenberg . He is a brilliant writer and a very smart entrepreneur, especially that he is able to come up with a book like this.

I'm excited that I will be able to share my most valuable knowledge in Amazon FBA through this book. I believe that there are great opportunities in Amazon FBA but only a few sellers grabbed the opportunity.

I'm sure that in this book, you'll get to know more about how Amazon works and how you can be a successful seller. But your future success will depend on the actions you take after reading this book.

The best secrets and practices will be revealed in this book and I encourage you to continue improving your Amazon FBA business with these new strategies that you will be learning in order to make greater profits.

Enjoy reading this book!

Dan Johnson

CHAPTER 1: WHAT IS AMAZON FBA?

Fulfillment by Amazon is a program that helps sellers and merchants boost sales through a world-class fulfillment service and expertise of Amazon. The fulfillment service includes picking, packing and shipping orders to customers that promise efficient delivery time and customer service.

Amazon has made selling as easy as possible with FBA by giving Amazon sellers the option of warehousing the inventory in Amazon fulfillment center.

Sellers have shown an increase in sales after using FBA and outperformed other competitors whose orders are not fulfilled by Amazon. More sellers on Amazon have adopted the FBA service wherein sellers can choose Amazon to ship its products directly to customers and offer Amazon Prime benefits.

Amazon FBA: Mastery:

4 Steps to Selling $6,000 per Month on Amazon FBA

By David Goldenberg & Dan Johnson

Published by Media Prestige eBook Publishing Company

© Copyright 2015

Table of Contents

Surely, using FBA is a game changer for Amazon sellers because inventories become eligible for Prime benefits. And eventually drives sales and benefit the customers as well

a. Why Amazon's Prime Subscribers Should Be Your Target?

Amazon's great success in selling has made millionaires through their e-commerce platform.

If you have been an Amazon seller for a long time, you may remember that it was in 2013 when over a billion units were sold worldwide. The rise makes up 40% of Amazon's total unit sales. Actually, Amazon's record shows 65% growth in the number of Amazon sellers using FBA service during that time.

So, why reach for Prime subscribers through FBA?

Amazon Prime subscribers are the loyal customers who enjoy greater value in the convenience of getting a product with a little extra payment for the quick service. Getting the Prime service for $99 per year, Amazon gives a free 2-day shipping with value added membership features and more fast-ship items to choose from.

Prime members shops at Amazon more frequently than nonmembers. More so, members shop across more categories, thus, they spend much more than nonmembers. Prime members enjoy various free or unlimited benefits such as videos, movies and ebooks but they are willing to buy when they can't get something for free on Amazon.

According to the study from Consumer Intelligence Research Partners (CIRP) in December 2013, Amazon Prime members spend an average of $1,340 annually while those that are non-Prime members spend an average of $529.

Just think of it this way, there are more than 20 million customers out there who are willing to spend more money, buy more often, and even buy more expensive products to get the most out of what they pay for the annual membership fee.

And so, these are the customers that you need to target.

b. How Amazon FBA Works?

With the presence of service providers like Amazon which takes care of the technical side of selling the products, Amazon sellers like you can focus now on your core strengths.

Additionally, the Amazon FBA program will provide you the picking, packing, shipping, returns and customer service by Amazon.

As the largest online marketplace, you'll have the access to a wider customer base by becoming an FBA seller. A survey in 2013 shows 73% of the participants have experienced a sales increase of 20% or greater after using FBA.

The illustration* below will show you how Amazon FBA works.

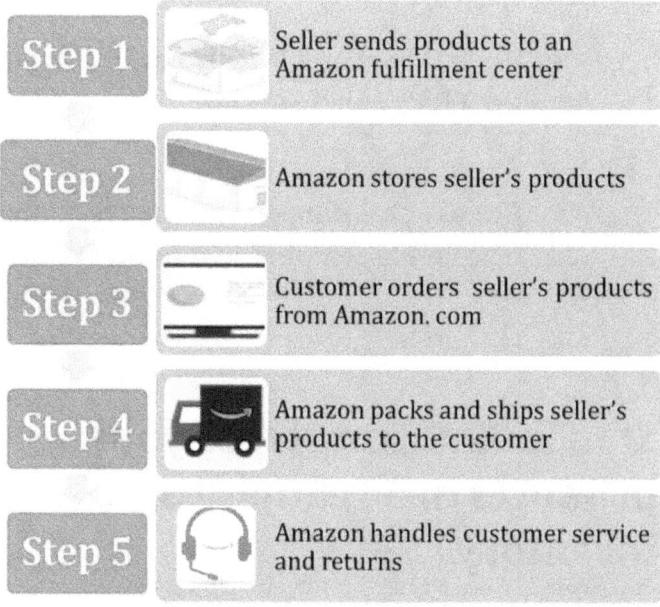

* *Source:* **Amazon FBA: Complete Guide: Make Money Online with Amazon FBA - The Fulfillment Amazon Bible**

Here is the step-by-step process in using Amazon FBA to fulfill orders:

Step 1: You send your products to Amazon's fulfillment centers.

- **Go to your Seller Central account** and upload your product listings. Take note of all or other parts of your inventory that can be fulfilled by Amazon.

- **Print labels** provided by Amazon or you may use FBA's **Label Service**.

- **Choose shipping options** between Amazon's discounted shipping or your own carrier.

Step 2: Amazon stores your products in a ready-to-ship inventory.

- **Amazon receives and scans your products** where they record Unit dimensions for storage.

- **Use Amazon's integrated tracking system** to monitor your inventory.

Step 3: Customers order your products and Amazon fulfills the order.

- **To check your listings**, it is ranked by price with no shipping costs. As an Amazon FBA seller, your products are eligible for free delivery on orders over $35.

- **Amazon Prime members have the option** to upgrade shipping options.

Step 4: Amazon picks, packs, and ships your products.

- **Amazon uses an advanced web-to-warehouse picking and sorting system** to locate your products. There are instances that customers can combine various orders of different products fulfilled by Amazon.

- **Orders are shipped to customers** using any method that Amazon chooses. Then, they provide tracking information for customers.

Step 5: Amazon handles customer service and returns.

- **Customers can contact Amazon** for customer service particularly in the case of delivery returns.

It's very simple. You sell the products, and Amazon ships it to the buyer.

Using the FBA service will cost you the **Fulfillment fees for orders** that depend on the category type and product size. The additional cost may be too high if you think about it, but with its favorable results, FBA can make more profit for you.

CHAPTER 2: HOW FBA CAN MAKE MORE MONEY IN YOUR POCKET?

First and foremost, you should not think that using Amazon FBA will just cost you additional fees. Definitely, it won't cause a cut on your margins. The FBA fees are compensated through the pricing strategy and higher sales volume.

In fact, selling with FBA is an advantage in facing tough competition in the Amazon marketplace.

a. How to know if you're right for FBA?

Sad to say, FBA may not be right for all businesses and sellers. To be a right match for FBA, you should meet some basic business characteristics.

Amazon FBA fits your business if you:

- Can invest in advanced inventory capital
- Have high volume and high margin
- Sells products at above $10 price
- Do not sell hazardous products or any Amazon restricted items
- Sells light and expensive or small, high margin items

Make yourself right with FBA by getting away from selling low volume and low margin products. However, there are some merchants who sell at the low margin but with high volume which can also be a good option. Also, it's advisable not to sell items under $10 because it can only eat up most of your profit margin.

You have to keep in mind the kinds of products when selling with Amazon FBA. Always check Amazon's guidelines of **Restricted Products** and **Hazardous Materials and Dangerous Items.** Any product that belongs to these categories will not be processed by FBA (e.g. explosives, aerosols, poisons, vehicle tires).

When using FBA, storage fees may cut your profit especially if you sell heavy and inexpensive items. So always keep in mind the storage fees when you sell products with FBA.

Again, FBA's storage cost will not be a burden if you do it with the right strategies.

b. Selling with FBA as a Competitive Advantage

With the competitive advantages of selling with FBA, you can make money at a higher rate compared to the earnings if you ship orders by yourself.

Here are the advantages of selling with FBA:

1 - Products are visible to Amazon Prime customers.
I'm talking about millions of loyal Prime members who are looking for FBA product listings because of the 2-day free shipping. Take note of the more favorable buying habits of Prime customers as compared to non-Prime customers. Using FBA will give you exposure to Prime members who buy more often and expensive items.

2 - Shipping price can be included in your total price.

What do I exactly mean by this? Since an item from FBA listing has no shipping cost, you can build the shipping price into the total price when comparing against the items Fulfilled by Merchant (FBM).

Let's say, an FBM product is sold at $15 with $5 shipping cost, then you can price the same product at $20 at no shipping cost. With FBA, your product will be shipped for 2-day free Prime shipping.

3 - Winning the Buy Box is possible.

Though it depends on the product category, you can have a competitive price with 10% higher than other sellers who are not using FBA and you can still win the Buy Box as you sell with FBA.

4 - Customers are willing to pay more for free 2-day shipping.

When same products have different shipping terms, most of the customers prefer the free 2-day shipping even if the price of the item is higher. It's only the FBA products that customers can get to have the free shipping.

5 - Customers feel fulfilled.

Amazon has a good reputation and it includes the customer service that they offer to customers. Amazon makes sure that the customers are happy with the service they provide. With FBA, your products will be shipped by Amazon and any return or refund will be attended by Amazon customer service.

Thus, a fulfilled customer is more willing to give great feedback on the purchased products. And these feedbacks can lead you to more customers.

6 - Can scale the business at an easier pace.
With FBA warehousing and customer services, there is no need for additional space for inventory and hire manpower when you plan to scale up your business.

7 - Expected higher sales volume.
There have been many sellers who showed a remarkable 20% sales increase after using FBA. Though, there are many factors to consider in determining how much sales increase you can achieve by selling with FBA, still you can expect a higher volume of sales when FBA is used.

These are the advantages that can earn you more money in your pocket as an Amazon seller with the use of FBA. These are the same reasons why you should use FBA so you can grow your business with an average of 45% as a successful seller.

CHAPTER 3: THE 2 SIMPLE WAYS TO BE A SMART FBA SELLER

As you sell on Amazon FBA, the fixed costs for warehouse rental and hired personnel may significantly reduce. But, using FBA will require you more focus on the product sourcing and inventory management.

To succeed in Amazon FBA, you should be able to execute a more strategic approach to handling the products you sell.

Furthermore, selling in Amazon with FBA is like investing in stock market. Why is it so?

Investing in the stock market requires selection of stocks and determination of how many shares to invest. While in selling FBA products, you have to select which products and how many units needs to be ordered. And both depend on how much capital you can invest and the strategies to make.

When selling with Amazon FBA, it will require you to choose the products that can perform well on Amazon to get profit from it. Then, the profits you make can be reinvested into other potential products. Thus, you have an opportunity to diversify your inventory and create more profit from your investments.

I know you have been selling on Amazon for a period of time and probably you have listed only the profitable products. I should say that with FBA selling, a thorough product sourcing and selection is required because not all products can make profits with FBA.

And so, only a little sophistication is needed for you to succeed on FBA.

When you use FBA, you have to be a SMARTER seller.... in two SIMPLE ways.

1 - Be active with inventory management.

You have to monitor the availability and stock level of your inventory at any given time. Remember always, to keep your bestsellers in a healthy inventory level. Make sure to dispose of your items that are not saleable because Amazon will only charge you with storage fees even for the non-selling stale products.

2 - Keep on scouting profitable products.
You need to add new products to your portfolio
and these should be the profitable items.
Expectedly, the more profitable products you have
the more profit you can generate.

Definitely, your product is a big factor in your
success in selling with FBA. Take advantage of the
inventory management tools provided in
Amazon Seller Central to help you manage
inventory. More so, there are different **product
sources** where you can scout new products. Being
a smart seller requires resourcefulness as well.

CHAPTER 4: HOW TO GROW WITH AMAZON FBA THROUGH PROFIT CYCLE?

From the time you started selling on Amazon, you may notice the increasing number of items listed on Amazon marketplace over time. This indicates that sellers are continuously arriving to compete and more active Amazon sellers are growing their businesses.

I believe that FBA is a factor of such growth. And the growth happens due to a repeating process of restocking the bestsellers, getting away of the unsalable items and scouting of new products.

To have a constant growth in your Amazon FBA business, your existing inventory should be evaluated and assessed in a strategic manner based on data. But be also ready to answer some questions because you need to assess your FBA operations.

First, let me discuss the most important concerns that a seller should focus on.

1 - Where's the Profit?

Basically, your profit depends on the products you sell and your sources. And so, it is important to identify which are the most profitable brands to sell with Amazon FBA. Review your sales data to check which of your product listings are generating profits on your portfolio.

If you haven't heard of the 80/20 rule especially in running a business, let me share it with you because it will guide you through the first step of the FBA profit cycle.

The 80/20 rule is named as the Pareto Principle which explains that 80% of the outputs are produced from 20% of the inputs. The principle can be applied in your Amazon FBA selling business when identifying the most profitable SKUs and suppliers from your list. Do this to cover the 20% of your inputs and when these products sell on Amazon, expect the 80% output to give you good results.

You should be able to identify which of the *SKUs you sell are generating more profit for you.

* Stock Keeping Unit (SKU) is a product you sell that has a distinct characteristic in its brand, variant, and size or packaging. No same SKU is considered to be the same because each SKU is distinguished from other items.

Additionally, other SKUs from your list that do not sell well should be liquidated so you can divert the investment to the most profitable products.

2 - How to Scout New Products?

Since you have found the brands and suppliers that give the highest profit, you should maintain your focus in scouting for more new products to the list that belong to the same brands and suppliers. In this sense, you are expanding your business through adding new profitable products and restocking the profitable SKUs.

I want to reiterate that stale inventory should be managed very well. Make sure to liquidate them regularly until such time that only the profitable items are listed.

3. How to make the Right Price?

There are various **repricing tools** that are available to Amazon sellers that you should use to ensure a real-time repricing of your products. The profitability of your products will depend on the repricing strategies you do that should be aligned with your business strategy.

Though you have the competitive advantage against the non-FBA sellers, I advise you not to compete with Fulfilled By Merchant prices because you may end up in an unprofitable price war.

4. How to have a Continued Growth?

Every sale you earn will indicate the result of the actions you took by practicing the 3 steps above. And so, it is necessary that you review product sales regularly. Make sure to restock the products that are creating sales since those are the products that are making you most of the profits.

When these concerns are addressed accordingly, it creates an FBA profit cycle. Repeat the process of identifying the most profitable SKUs, scouting new products and strategizing reprice of products and then review your sales.

Do all the steps all over again so you'll succeed with Amazon FBA. The proper way to do it is to list the right product with the right price and restock the product on time.

You probably still have questions on how you can profit or how can a profit cycle earn you highest profits ever with Amazon FBA.

It's necessary that these strategies should be practiced to earn big profits in Amazon FBA through a continuous cycle.

Here's the 4-step process which I have been very excited to share with you. Through this cycle, you'll be able to create more income with Amazon FBA.

STEP 1: Identify the Most Profitable Brands and Suppliers

Have you thought of your bestseller items? But have you ever thought of the products that are profitable? If ever you know the profitable SKUs, do you already have a time table in reordering each item so there would be no out-of-stock?

Do you have stale inventories and have you considered how much FBA fees are spent for its storage? These are the most critical questions that you should address as you start a profit cycle.

There is a common mistake that sellers do when it comes to optimizing the FBA selling business. It's not merely managing the bestselling products. It's also the constant identification of the most profitable brands and suppliers and the monitoring of potential stale inventories through time.

Thus, assessing each SKU is necessary.

Here's a checklist that can guide you to evaluate your brands and suppliers.

1 - Determine the sellout rate.
You need to monitor how many units are sold and if you are profiting from it, assess if it is enough to continue listing the SKU.

2 - Determine the profit margin.
In selling a business, profit margin relies on the business strategy. Usually, sellers go for higher profit margin, and I can say that it is preferable. But then again, it depends on your strategy because there are some sellers who make low margins with high volume business.

3 - Observe the price trends.

Price competition is normally disadvantageous to your business. Whenever competition leads to a price war, you have to be extra watchful on pricing your items. The items that are driven below your lowest acceptable price are definitely not worth investing and restocking.

4 - Decide on reorder quantity.

Determining how many units to reorder is a crucial decision to make especially when each SKU differs on reorder quantity.

There are data that you need to review to be able to get your *Reorder Quantity (RQ)*. Here's the list of data you have to consider:

- **Lead-Time(LT)** - How many days will you expect to receive the products after placing your order?

- **Basic Stock (BS)** - How many days of inventory are kept in a normal period?

- **Safety Stock (SS)** - How many days of inventory are kept in case of emergency?

- **Sales per Day (SPD)** - What is the average number of items sold per day?

After determining the above data, use the formula below as a guide:

RQ = [LT + BS + SS] x SPD

5 - Prepare your Purchase Order.
Each profitable SKU will start making money with the right number of units to reorder. Prepare your purchase order according to the suggested formula I discussed in #4.

With this basic framework, you can now evaluate your existing FBA inventory. Remember that profiting from selling with Amazon FBA does not end in evaluating the existing inventory.

Evaluating products are essential because it is very rare that a product will sell at the same rate within several months. And so, a constant scouting and testing of new FBA products should be done as well. You can't tell when a competitor will come out with a lower price or possibly Amazon will sell the same item as yours. In these instances, you have to be prepared with new products on your list.

Now, it's time to assess if you have stale inventory because it can be a silent killer to your FBA business. Are you aware that if ever you have stale inventory, it's actually a loss of money in terms of fees and opportunities?

Stale inventory is disadvantageous to your business because:

- You'll be charged with semi-annual fees by Amazon depending on cubic volume.

- Your capital will be tied up wherein you can't use it to invest in new products or for other operational costs.

- Items that are seasonal, trending and perishable will only incur fees if no action to dispose or liquidate is taken.

Whenever you see some stale inventory on your list, try to check your options. You may either sell them at a loss or communicate with the supplier to return. However, you will be charged with return fees by Amazon if you opt to return the product to your supplier.

STEP 2: Scout New Products

Initially, when you scout new products it doesn't require going too far from what you already have. Save your time in scouting by checking your existing most profitable brands and suppliers.

Listing of new brands is one of the biggest challenges of a seller, and so it is advisable that you start with the existing networks to optimize the relationships.

Try to look into some items that your supplier carries and determine if you can sell them. Definitely, seeking other opportunities in your existing suppliers can make your business grow.

Here is a guide on how to evaluate new products to sell on Amazon.

To Do #1: Check if Amazon is a seller of the item that you wish to sell.
You can proceed to evaluate the item if Amazon is not a seller.

To Do #2: Review the Sales rank of the item.
In choosing new products, it is recommended to check the top level category rank of the item on Amazon. If the rank is below 5,000, then you can consider adding the product and continue the evaluation process.

To Do #3: Determine the presence of other FBA sellers.
This will give you an idea of the competition level of a particular product. If there are few or no other FBA sellers, then proceed to the next "To Do" step. Still, current competition should not prevent you from pursuing a product because more FBA sellers only show a demand for the product.

To Do #4: Assess if the product is profitable to list on Amazon FBA.
You do profit calculation whenever you scout a product.

Use your current profit calculation formula if you have any. You can also use the **Amazon FBA Revenue Calculator** that can provide you the fulfillment and real-time costs comparisons between your own fulfillment and Amazon FBA offers.

Here's a sample calculation that you may use:

Profit = [Buy Box Price - (Wholesale Cost + FBA Fee + Amazon Fee + Commission % + Shipping cost)] x Quantity to Order

To Do #5: Evaluate if the profit is adequate for your business.

You may set your product profitability requirements before deciding to sell and base your decision on the size of your business. If the profitability of the item is adequate for the business, then make a purchase order of this new product and start selling it with Amazon FBA. Otherwise, do not add the item and just look into other products to evaluate.

Believe it or not! Scouting and listing the best brands and suppliers that are identified to have the highest profits can turn up your sales volume and earn you more income.

STEP 3: Strategize the Right Price of the Products

Now that you have evaluated a new product to sell on Amazon FBA, the next step is to ensure that the selling price will earn you high profits. To do so, you need to have the right strategy to price it right.

At this stage, you should aim to take control of getting the Buy Box. There can be a lot of challenges in winning the Buy Box, but more opportunities to profit will come when you reprice strategically.

If you haven't used any repricer tool or software, there are various tools available to Amazon sellers such as **RepriceIt, ScanPower, Sellery** and **Teikametrics**. Repricer tool can make repricing an easy task, but you should think about your repricing strategies thoroughly so your sales will increase and your business will grow.

You should be watchful in using repricer tools and strategizing the right price of your products.

Here's what other sellers are mistakenly doing and thinking which does not help them in making good strategies to earn more profit:

- Sellers are pricing a product for competitive advantages.

- Sellers consider all repricers as the same.

- When price rules and seller's strategy don't match.

Most of the sellers struggle in winning the Buy Box because of its subtle and unusual changes over time. Some sellers reprice the items with higher price whenever a competitor has no stocks or there is no other seller of the item. There are also instances when a seller increases or lowers the price depending on who fulfills the orders, whether by Amazon or by Merchant.

Having the competitive advantage over other sellers should not drive a seller to reprice a product because price rules against an FBA seller would not apply to another FBA seller. The common mistake of sellers is repricing a product to have the advantage and compete with other sellers just to win the Buy Box. But, repricing only requires understanding the behavior of Amazon's Buy Box.

STEP 4: Review Results, Restock Products and Repeat the Steps

The most crucial step in the profit cycle is to ensure continued growth in selling with Amazon FBA.

At this stage, you should review how your products perform and watch out when Amazon would not allow a listing of a certain product or your supplier would not want you to list the product on Amazon. If you do not act offensively on how Amazon and other sellers behave, you'll end up frustrated when sales are cut.

Every seller recognizes the intense competition in Amazon, isn't it? In fact, there is no guarantee that your bestseller item today could remain a bestseller the next few days. And so, it is recommended to keep an eye on every item that sells, makes a profit, and the inventory that may generate extra storage fees.

Upon sales review of each item, make sure to restock the profitable products and keep scouting products first from the existing brands and suppliers. Act on the stale inventory and repeat the process from Step 1. Your business will grow when you do all these tasks consistently.

CHAPTER 5: WRAP UP: THE 5 BEST LEARNING ON AMAZON FBA

Being an advanced Amazon seller should not limit you to learn more about selling on Amazon and how you can raise profit and grow your business.

Here is a wrap-up of what you have learned from this book:

Learning #1: More business opportunities for retailers are offered by Amazon, being the world's largest e-commerce platform.

Learning #2: A program like Amazon FBA is the best option to automate picking, packing, shipping and customer service tasks.

Learning #3: The most preferred target is the Prime subscribers. They are the customers who buy more and willing to pay an extra cost for free shipping and convenience.

Learning #4: A more strategic approach to product sourcing and inventory management is needed when selling with Amazon FBA.

Learning #5: A 4-step profit cycle should be followed to be able to achieve consistent and long-term profits in selling with Amazon FBA.

The 4-step profit cycle to follow:
- Identify the most profitable brands and suppliers

- Source new products

- Strategize the right price of the product

- Review results, restock products and repeat the steps

Heads up my friend! Practice these lessons to have a more productive outcome. As you continue selling on Amazon, mastering FBA can lead you to earn a greater profit and a growing selling business.

CHAPTER 6: 25 BEST KEPT SECRETS OF SUCCESSFUL SELLERS ON AMAZON

Definitely, there are more things to learn in Amazon FBA to be a successful seller. Here are more tips for you. These tips are from one of the best-selling books by Dan Johnson: **Amazon FBA: Complete Guide**.

As an Amazon seller, joining the Fulfillment by Amazon could be the best part of the online selling business that helps you boost sales and earn income. I know how important it is to be guided from the beginning so as to avoid setbacks and mistakes along the way. And so, I thought of sharing some secrets that made the success of other Amazon sellers.

Here are the best-kept secrets that you deserve to know:

Secret #1: Review and follow Amazon's rules and guidelines.

Sellers who continually grow with selling on Amazon are those who are comfortable with the **rules and regulations** of Amazon. It is recommended that you browse in the **Help section** to get more detailed "how-to" instructions or contact them whenever there are issues unclear to you. Aside from the rules and regulations, take advantage of the **resources page for FBA sellers** for more guidance.

- **Amazon Rules and Regulations page:** https://goo.gl/eeuMzY

- **Help Section page:** http://goo.gl/AU2vPK

- **FBA Sellers Resources page:** http://goo.gl/hkXPvy

Secret #2: Work on becoming an Amazon Featured Merchant.

The biggest advantage of being a featured merchant on Amazon is to have the chance of getting the "Buy Box" on Amazon, which provides you with default sales. It only means that you get the sale when someone clicks the "Add to Cart" button for the product.

The fact is that Amazon doesn't advice any guidelines on how to become a featured merchant; and so, it is the seller's initiative to discover what it takes to become one.

However, the must-have of a featured merchant is to have good feedbacks aside from having a right seller account and good product sales.

Secret #3: Flexibility with pricing strategy and promotions.

Putting your products on sale may occur, but sellers ensure that it is done to get a little more sales rank. Other reasons than that may not be beneficial to you. If you tend to lower your price just to be able to compete with others, then, it would not help your business. It is rather preferable to play with little competition.

And when you need to earn more profit, be flexible and try to raise your prices, as small as 3% increase. Definitely, it could contribute a little to your income.

Secret #4: Decide on your margins.

Successful sellers are those running the business to generate income and not to cost them money. Determining what your margin needs careful decision together with identifying every fee involved. Since this is a critical part of the business, the Apps or tools I have listed in this book can help you evaluate and reprice your products to come up with profitable margins.

Secret #5: Look out for marketing opportunities within Amazon.

Amazon is often offering different marketing opportunities to make an easy selling on Amazon. Taking advantage of it and using the tools provided by Amazon would open up new strategies for the business.

Secret #6: Take advantage of the holidays.

One of the greatest times of the year for businesses is during holidays when sales possibly increase up to five times the average sales. And so, sellers are getting ready for these periods with a handful of inventory. Successful sellers are able to forecast the demand for their product so not to have excessive inventory by the time that the occasion has passed.

As you go along, try to keep a seasonal profile forecast and eventually you can refer to it year after year. You need to be familiar with your peak seasons so you can get ready and prepare your inventory.

Secret #7: Handle your package and label with care.

This is the part of the business that shouldn't be missed out.

The products must be shipped to Amazon successfully. This means to provide proper and enough packing in shipping products to Amazon. Basically, it will ensure that your products won't be damaged, even if when products are accidentally dropped.

One of the best wraps to use is the bubble wrap or Kraft Paper. You may use the 1/2" paper size, but adding extra packing is advisable for heavier products. Never use a loose-fill packaging such as packing peanuts because Amazon doesn't like such packaging material.

Secret #8: Use the Amazon's Seller Central Reports.

Inventory and Sales reports are necessary for running a selling business and good thing about being an Amazon seller is that there are reports available when you access your Amazon seller account. Make use of these reports in evaluating your business and how to improve it.

There are reports where you can determine how much money your products make, as well as what your inventory level is. Knowing the results of promotions you have listed and the reasons for customer refunds and returns are essential information, which you can download from Amazon's Seller Central. Most importantly, use the reports when forecasting sales so you'll not run out of your products.

Secret #9: Consider space and business size to select products.

Selling takes time to research, but there are times that it only takes common sense to decide. Managing inventory starts from finding a good product to storing at your own place for a short period, then shipping to Amazon.

If you have no available big space and you want to sell mattress or sofas, would you rent another place just to accommodate such large items? I don't think it's a good idea unless your cash flow can manage additional warehouse and shipping costs and can markup your product so high to earn profits.

Secret #10: Use the "perfect" fulfillment service.

The best-kept secret of Amazon sellers is using the Amazon FBA that provides the fulfillment service. It only takes a few bulk shipments to Amazon as compared to individually shipping orders to your customers. It simply frees up your time.

Secret #11: Be proactive in managing inventory.

Maintaining a healthy inventory on Amazon can make a good sales rank of your products.

Amazon Sales Ranks are based on the quantity of the sale at a particular time. Consequently, non-stock affects the sales rank of your product because each day that your product makes no sale, sales rank drops every day. To avoid running out of stocks, you should manage your inventory proactively. Use the Amazon Manage Inventory tools to your advantage. Consider the time it takes to order from suppliers until it is shipped to you and the time you ship the inventory to Amazon. In this way, you can estimate when to start replenishing your inventory especially when the holiday season is approaching.

Secret #12: Give feedback on customer inquiry immediately.

Whenever a customer has questions, Amazon expects the seller to respond to customer questions within 24 hours. If you don't want to get a demerit on your account, you'd better answer customer communications quickly. To do this, log on your Seller Central page and set up the automation to receive customer questions on your email so you can also answer inquiries whenever you're not logged on Amazon.

Secret #13: Check the UPC codes when listing products thoroughly.

Make sure to double check and read the full description and specs of the products before listing to Amazon carefully.

You must be aware that there are manufacturers who do not change UPC codes whenever they make changes on the features of a product. When this happens and the item you sell is not the latest version of the product, expect returns with bad feedback from your buyers because of inappropriate items. And so, looking at the images of the product is not enough. When adding a product on Amazon, be responsible for listing on Amazon the "exact" product-- you must sell the 100% identical product.

Secret #14: Prepare accurate product description.

The product description is normally the customer's basis of buying decisions. The customer will notice even a slight difference between the description and the actual item when delivered. Describing a product accurately is what successful sellers practically do so that it won't lead to possible returns or negative feedbacks.

Secret #15: Get more feedback and product reviews.

Expect that Amazon buyers do not leave feedback naturally after purchasing a product. And usually, customers are more motivated to give feedback when they have a bad experience with the product. What sellers normally do is to ask customers to make a review or feedback because one of the most effective ways to market a product is having more feedback.

Whenever a customer expressed that they liked the product, you can thank them through email and include a link where they can write a product review for what they purchased.

To help you out on this, there is a third party service called **FeedbackFive**, which is designed to manage feedback scores by soliciting feedback from customers, reviewing the received feedbacks whether negative or neutral feedback. The software also monitors the trends and able to accept a request for removal of negative feedbacks.

FeedbackFive website: www.feedbackfive.com

The emails are sent to customers automatically with a link to click on and leave feedback. With a cost from $9.99 to $99.90 per month, depending on the plan and features, you'll be able to get more feedback.

Secret #16: Follow Amazon image guidelines.

Buyers are enticed to buy a product usually through the product images shown. Product images help describe the items you are selling and provide a useful information to customers. Notwithstanding the large size of images for the use of customers, following the Amazon's **photo guidelines and requirements** must be a priority. Currently, all photos are scaled to 500 x 500 pixels and photos that do not have a 1:1 dimension ratio are padded with white space on the shorter sides.

Amazon's photo guidelines and requirements:
http://goo.gl/cNLFGa

Secret #17: Use Just in Time (JIT) Inventory Management.

This refers to replenishing your inventory to Amazon just before it runs out. Doing this would minimize the time that Amazon stores your inventory; thus, storage fees are reduced. You can manage this by setting the Replenishment Alert as a Manage Inventory tool, so you'll be notified whenever your inventory has reached its threshold.

Secret #18: Consider your Average Selling Price (ASP) in computing fees and profit margins.

In any business, the goal is to minimize percentage costs and increase profit margins. And so, the higher the average selling price, the higher is the profit margin while costs percentage gets lower.

For example, a fixed Order Handling fee for non-media products is $1 and the Pick & Pack fee is $1.02, with a total of $2.02 fixed fee for every unit. If you will be selling the item at $15, the $2.02 fee is equivalent to 13.47% of your margin. But, if you raise the price at $28, then the percentage fees will only take 7.2% of your margin.

It is advisable that you look for an item that you can sell at a price that ranges from your average selling price. And, the average selling price must take a minimal percentage of the fees.

Secret #19: Label items and shipments correctly.

There will always be an instance that you'll mislabel an item when you prepare for shipment to fulfillment center especially if you're not able to establish a process to double check each product and boxes. As your inventory increases, the possibility of mixing up labels may increase as well. And so, make sure to double check labeling so it won't mess up your shipments, reach your customer and get a negative feedback from the buyer. In packing your product, it is also recommended that you can see the item inside the package as a way to double check the items when you box them to ship.

Secret #20: Pack shipments to Amazon correctly.

Give an extra effort to pack shipments meticulously to avoid delays and penalty fees. Amazon's packaging and shipping requirements are strictly followed when sending items to fulfillment centers. It ensures that items will not be damaged, be processed and fulfilled efficiently.

Look out on the most critical requirements to pack items such as:

- Correct size box for the unit (use rigid box with flaps intact)

- Wrapping of all items separately (do not use string or paper over-wrap)

- Strong tape (designed for shipping)

- Clear single address label (with complete delivery and return information)

- Two inches cushioning between each unit and inside the box (do not use loose Styrofoam pellets for void filler)

- Re-used boxes may be used (be sure to remove previous shipping labels and any scannable barcodes)

- Do not bundle boxes using taping, elastic, extra straps or bagging

- Always review the Quick Reference Guide

Secret #21: Act on negative feedbacks.

Neutral or negative feedbacks on your products can automatically lose your featured seller status. If it falls below 95%, Amazon may cancel your account. Sellers take action to remove negative feedbacks through reaching out to the customers. What you can do is to immediately email the customer to extend your sincerest apology on what they have experienced from your product. Along with the apology could be an Amazon gift card as a token of sincerity, a $10 gift card is advisable. Usually, the customer sends back to extend gratitude to you and that is the best time to explain how the error occurred, then, you can request to remove the feedback.

This won't guarantee a 100% positive response from the customers, but surely you can get over a half of your negative feedbacks.

Secret #22: Increase sales through Buy Box

This is the page that is shown whenever a buyer clicks on one of the results that buyer searched on. The majority of the sales are earned through the "buy box" that is why sellers work on winning the buy box.

Here's the list of what sellers do to win the buy box.

- ***Listing products with the lowest price and shipping.*** A seller who maintains good standing and lists the lowest price including the shipping is able to make its product in the buy box ahead of other sellers. However, Amazon assumes that shipping cost is zero for FBA sellers because of the free 2-day shipping for Amazon Prime members whose shipment has a minimum of $35.

- **Selling an item as the only seller.** Automatically, you'll win the buy box if there are no other sellers of an item you're selling. So, go and find that unique product to sell on Amazon.

- **Creating bundling items as per Amazon's** bundling policy. There is a creative way to make a unique item and that is through product bundling. It could be different items bundled together or an item packed to make a set of a new product. Just make sure to bundle in the media category with any item from other categories and not bundling same media category.

  Amazon's bundling policy page:
  http://goo.gl/EiweNH

Secret #23: Negotiate selling exclusivity with suppliers.

It is possible that a seller can be an exclusive seller of a particular manufacturer or supplier.

Sellers usually scout for manufacturers in wholesale trade shows to negotiate selling exclusivity to Amazon since in most instances owners are available in the booth.

Here's what you should know and communicate with company owners when you see a good product at the trade show:

- Do they sell on Amazon or other online retail sites?

- Offer them to look out for anyone who undercut their brand online

- Assure them not to lower the prices below what their retailers sell

- Let them know you'll get their approval for all images and product description to use on listing their product

- Provide some references of other companies you sell exclusively if any

Secret #24: Use the Amazon keywords wisely.

For any online business, keywords can make money for someone who knows how to use it.

These are words or phrases that are typed in by Amazon buyers in the search box when they find products. It is good that Amazon provides a keyword field when sellers create a listing. You should learn how to use the keyword field that Amazon provides.

Here is a guide on how you can use Amazon keyword wisely:

- **Repeat keywords** from your bullets and descriptions in the keyword field but not in the keyword field of the title.

- **Use related competitor's product name** as keywords.

- **Use word misspellings as one of the keywords**, although Amazon corrects spelling, there are often popular misspellings used as keywords.

- **Think of other words that people might type** in when searching a product like yours. Sometimes people use different terms like foot "cream" or foot "lotion."

- **Use two different forms of the word** such as splitting into two words or putting a space in between. For example, use Coolpix and Cool pix as keywords.

Secret #25: Use Amazon FBA to fulfill multi-channel orders.

It is a good step to fulfill multi-channel orders using Amazon FBA if you sell your products or plan to sell to other channels like eBay or Etsy. Shipping charge may be less than UPS or Priority mail. You can create Fulfillment Order where you can fill in the buyer information. If later you want to automate fulfilling multi-channel orders, you may use **AutoMCF**. It is a service that connects your marketplace listing to FBA that automatically process when an item sells on eBay, sync inventory and get the item from the FBA inventory. This tool spares you from manual order entry and ship tracking.

AutoMCF Website: www.automcf.com

I know that any selling business makes a tremendous income to those who put every effort and time into productive activities. Reviewing these secrets once in a while could make a difference on how to handle selling on Amazon. These are bits of important aspects of the Amazon business operations, which are practically done by successful Amazon sellers.

Leave a Book Review

Tell us what you think
Did you learn something from this book? Tell other readers what you think about this book by leaving a book review.

Write a Book Review: https://goo.gl/Uba8F7

My New Book

Hi, Friend!

I just released a new and more advanced book called **Amazon FBA: Complete Expert Guide.** This book tackles more **secrets** on *how you can Private Label your products, how to deal with the manufacturers,* and *how to grow your Amazon FBA business.* It will be helpful if you could also purchase this book for your own study and reference since this book deals with more advanced topics in more detail.

Amazon FBA: Complete Expert Guide book page: http://goo.gl/Gs7ZJt

Once again, thank you for purchasing this book. And as a token of thanks, I'm giving you, for FREE, the first chapter of my new book. Have a wonderful reading. Thanks a lot!

– Dan Johnson.

Book Description

Amazon FBA is the answer to the problem that all online sellers undergo. With Amazon FBA, you can achieve a consistent and swift shipping service that you do not need to bother with. They do all the picking, packing, shipping and many more processes for you! What about the warehousing space? Well, they cover that as well.

Imagine. All this information placed in one book.

This book does not only solve the problem encountered with shipping services or warehousing services. It also dives into every aspect you should consider with every product. From which products you should consider selling, international markets you can sell in, placing you in the search engine even as a new seller, tips on promoting your products and even the right way to price your products so there's no chance of bankruptcy.

With the use of this Amazon FBA e-book, you have stumbled on the best how-to; guidebook there is to increase your selling experience and success rate to the maximum level!

Amazon FBA is the ultimate guide for online sellers, both for the already established substantial and highly reputable retail firms, for the little, just-started online retail stores and everything in between.

It is based on the opportunity of selling your products online through the use of Fulfillment by Amazon, otherwise known as Amazon's FBA. Amazon, the genius that they are, has come up with a brilliant way in aiding your insufficient online business in becoming the best of the best! They pack, pick and ship all your products that your customers have ordered to lessen your headache.

Letting this opportunity go may lose your opportunity in beating the competitor's that you have dreamed of surpassing. The long awaited ultimate book to success in online selling has arrived.

CHAPTER 1: WHAT IS FULFILLMENT BY AMAZON (FBA)?

So what is this game-changing way of selling your products you ask?

Amazon has been able to innovate and create one of the most advanced fulfillment networks in the world, with the smart idea of contributing to help other people's businesses in the process.

It's a service that basically has Amazon store the products that you sell in their fulfillment centers.

They will be able to do everything from picking, packing and shipping your product with provided customer services.

This has supported so many businesses already, as it helps you scale your business and be able to reach the customers you weren't able to before. A survey was done in 2014 showing that 71% of FBA respondents have reported that their unit sales have increased to 20% more on Amazon.com once they have joined.

This can help your business too.

Let's take this example:

Back in the day, if you wanted to ship items to your customers, you would have to do it one at a time rather than all at once. This meant that as business and sales got better, then you would have to hire employees and more warehouse space. Basically, you'd have a headache.

What Fulfillment by Amazon had done, is that they had taken away all the headache of past problems and provided a simple solution to the problem: *You will ship your products in bulk to Amazon and Amazon will be the ones to pack and ship each individual order that you have received for you*

Isn't that amazing?

That Isn't The Only Benefit Of FBA

But, simply disposing of the headache of shipping isn't any different to all the other fulfillment centers out there that provide the same service Amazon does.

Now you're asking: *What's the big deal with Amazon's fulfillment centers then?*

Well, you don't just have all your products in one place and being shipped for you, but your sales will definitely jump, not just sissy kids jump, but like really a jump when in the use of FBA.

Why Does Sales Increase?

The reason your sales increase when using Amazon's FBA is that now your products can qualify under the Amazon's Free Super Saver Shipping. This basically means that Amazon will be able to offer to your customer free shipping when there is a purchased done over $25

It's not over because Amazon will also be able to offer their Amazon Prime members Free, Two-day shipping on all of your products.

Now, if you think about it, as you are shopping online do you think you would prefer to buy from a seller that is able to offer you a 2-day shipping for Free? People would die for that 2-day Free Shipping. If it weren't there, there would be more of a chance that your customers would just pass on your products. In the end, most of your potential customers would be passing, due to the hassle of adding shipping fee and long shipping time.

Fulfillment by Amazon is able to remove this hurdle along with your headache.

This Business Does Not Sleep

Since Amazon has the responsibility of shipping your products to all your customers, it has to work 24 hours a day in order to make sure that your orders go out fast and can be delivered on time to customers.

You are able to even go on vacation and your business will be able to run on autopilot for you, orders will be able to come in and products will go out as you sip on that Pina Colada.

A Growing Internet Business

Instead of attaining the expensive warehouse space that you need and all the employees you need to hire in order to ship your orders, you are able to work at home and be able to ship your products to Amazon in bulk.

You know what? You can even have any imported goods shipped directly to the Amazon fulfillment centers.

This type of business model allows you to grow rapidly without the need for all the tremendously expensive warehouse space and equipment that would add on to the costs of your business.

You are also able to use this model as a way to manage and ship the orders that your customers have placed in other online markets such as eBay, Buy.com, and others.

What Are The Products That You Are Allowed To Ship To Amazon?

Amazon may have started out as an online outlet for selling books, but it has definitely improved how it was before.

People can now buy jewelry, lawnmowers, beds, electronics and even exercise equipment. You want it; just name it.

You have the ability to ship even media items like books and non-media items like toys, home or garden items and much, much more.

The Fulfillment By Amazon Fees

The Fulfillment by Amazon fees are considerably low, which makes it definitely beneficial for those who have just started out in this business.

The fees may be updated from time to time and change, but the following are what you could expect:

- Fee for Picking (Per Order) = Approximately $1

- Fee for Packing (Per Order) = Approximately $1

- Weight-based Fee (Per Order) = Approximately $0.40 for every pound being shipped to a customer

- Storage Fee = Approximately $0.45 for every cubic foot of storage space that you may need to attain

- Inbound Freight = What it may cost you to ship your products to Amazon

- What's great about inbound freight fee is that Amazon will support you by partnering you up with them on shipping; this means that you will be able to use their shockingly low shipping rates.

All you have to do is to tell Amazon how big and heavy your package will be and the website will produce a label for you to be able to place on your box.

Easy and Simple, don't you think?

To see Amazon FBA's latest fee charges, please check **FBA Fulfillment Fees** page.

FBA Fulfillment Fees page: http://goo.gl/wi1d8g

Does FBA Work Only For People Working From Home?

Of course not!

There are even businesses that have already been in the business of selling online and had already been able to sell thousands upon thousands of products in their online stores even though they weren't using FBA. After joining the FBA program, their sales and business had increased tremendously.

Is It Possible To Have A Right And A Wrong Way To Use FBA?

Yes, there is.

This is more in the sense that there are strategies that would definitely help your business when using the FBA tactic and there are strategies that would just bring your business down.

Here's an example:

It would be most unfortunate for you and your business if you had decided to purchase vast amounts of products and ship it to the Amazon fulfillment centers just to realize that numerous amounts of other people have already done the same thing you did.

You need to be able to think strategically when you come into this business; you can't just go in blindly.

Ask yourself this: *'What can you and your business provide that no one else has already?'* or *'What can you sell to be unique from all the other businesses?'*

If you want to be able to achieve the different from the usual, then list all the products you have noticed that has not already been in the FBA and you will be able to benefit immensely if you are able to follow this strategy.

Once you take a look at the products that no one else is selling then you are able to sell your products without the worry of the competition within your online market.

Make sure you look for those items that differentiate you from the rest and can be considered desirable to all your potential customers and you will be able to gain so much more sales than you could have ever considered gaining.

a. Reasons To Choose Amazon For Selling

There are numerous other online markets to sell from, Amazon and eBay are two examples. They are both highly successful platforms for selling although they have differences in their operation, shopping experience.

Sellers may get confused as to where and who to go to sell, here's a quick guide as to why choosing Amazon would be most advantageous to your business compared to the rest.

1 - Elegance And Simplicity

Amazon has a very simplistic and organized selling platform in the industry. Comparing Amazon and the other online selling platforms, the others may have a longer process to go through just to get selling. Amazon's web store interface is also elegant and simple to use which will make your buyer's shopping experience a more enjoyable one.

2 - Attaining Fulfillment Without The Hassle

When using another online market platform, it would be up to you as the seller to see that your buyer gets what they paid for. This basically means that you will either have to create and maintain relationships between fulfillment partner(s) or that you would have to handle your own fulfillment (all the inventory, packaging, and shipping) all on your own.

When in Amazon, you can use their Fulfillment by Amazon, just send everything to Amazon with no cost and let them deal with your headache.

3 - Reduced Overhead

The way Amazon has created its system does not just provide the fulfillment platform, but it allows provides the opportunity to reduce their overhead expenses.

Since, in Amazon, you don't need to produce your own listing or continuously re-list your items on Amazon. Your maintenance overhead levels, as time goes by, will reduce.

The same things happen for the communication time since the buyers and sellers rarely need any communication.

4 - Better Visibility As A Smaller Seller

As a seller that may be just starting out in an online marketing platform, you may be one of those people buried at the end of the search list and covered by all those top-sellers or those that high-level feedbacks due to the innovation of the best match search system.

What Amazon does is that they have created a system that when buyers are searching for an item, the sellers that are shown are rotated. This allows for the new sellers to gain exposure. Since the buyers that go to Amazon, don't technically need to evaluate the sellers then there is almost always guaranteed sale.

5 - Be Where The Industry Has Growth

The online marketplace platform of Amazon has been growing much more rapidly year-by-year than that of any other online marketplace platforms is growing.

So, if you want to be in action then Amazon is for you.

From what this chapter has mentioned, Amazon has a lot to offer than that of any other online marketing platforms.

However, Amazon isn't for everyone; we all have our own dissenting opinions on its operation. But here are just a couple of points that will help you contemplate on the possible advantages you can reap from Amazon.

Amazon isn't Amazon today without the immense marketing and advertising strategies; a pinnacle of technological commerce in the modern era. Amazon is growing in consumers and members each day reaching out to various parts of the globe. One of the apparent benefits of selling on Amazon is the millions of people and markets it is currently attracting. It presents you with open access to sell your products in all five Amazon marketplaces in the safety of your home. There are more chances of you selling your product here than at the local mart. More exposure, more consumers, more money.

It's completely understandable that you're just not used to doing things online and prefer more tangible methods of earning money. However, everyone is using Amazon to expand their business horizons, either surf the wave of revenue or be attached to traditional concepts of business. Amazon is constantly upgrading to keep up with the dynamic world.

It's not to say that you should immediately shut your website or store or any personal retail outside of Amazon; the situation is relative. If your website offers more income to your pockets, then so be it. Nevertheless, Amazon will give you, even more, opportunities on top of your standard income.

The idea of it excites you, otherwise, you wouldn't be reading about what you can benefit from Amazon. There's no costly rent in comparison to tangible stores, you don't even need to worry about location. You can save the hassle of marketing your products and have people familiarize your brand. As long as you follow these rules and have the ethical and positive approach to this business, you're good to go.

Perhaps you doubt the faithfulness of the people you transact with; scammers, fraud and all. Have no fear. Amazon's security is something it should boast with novel ways of protecting you and your customers - from strict regulations on timely payments to traceable shipment. Disobedience to the rules will either lower your status to make it difficult to conduct business or ban you completely. Amazon has little tolerance to fraudulent schemes to create a protected working environment for all.

You may think that the added fees on top of your products don't leave you enough room for profit. You may believe that in the end, you'll be the one making a loss. I beg to differ. Amazon has generated components to make it as trouble-free as possible. Features, like the fixed price of the Pro Merchant Subscriptions, actually gives you a heads up on your expenses calculations. The Fulfillment by Amazon (FBA) offers a great deal of ways to increase your sales, customer service available in the local language and Amazon warehouses that stores your products for you. It's a win-win situation.

b. How Does It Work?

Now you have an idea of what Fulfillment by Amazon is and the numerous amounts of benefits that it can provide for you and your business.

How exactly does it work? The way that Fulfillment by Amazon works has been mentioned previously, although, we will now go on an in-depth explanation of how it goes about its process.

In simple words: **Your business sells the items and Amazon ships it**.

Here are steps on how to use the FBA:

STEP #1: Send All Your Products To Amazon
All of the products from new to used are first sent to Amazon's fulfillment centers.

Here are the sub-steps provided to proceed to send your products to Amazon's fulfillment centers.

- You can do this by first uploading your listings to the Seller Central

- After that, you allow Amazon to fulfill either all or part of your inventory listing

- Print the PDF labeling either provided by Amazon or you can use the Fulfillment by Amazon's label service

- Use the discounted shipping that Amazon provides or you can select your own carrier of choice.

STEP #2: Amazon Will Store All Your Products
Once all your products have been sent to Amazon, they will then catalog your items and store your products in their ready-to-ship inventory

This is how it works:
- Once Amazon has received your products, they will then scan your inventory

- Unit dimensions are then provided to be able to accommodate the storage space needed

- For those who want to monitor their inventory placed in the Amazon's fulfillment center, there is an integrated tracking system established by Amazon.

STEP #3: Customers Will Place Orders For Your Products

Customers who have placed orders directly on Amazon will be fulfilled by Amazon.

- Your listings on Amazon will be ranked by the prices presented with no shipping costs added since those items are entitled to free shipping for purchases that are over $35*.

- For those customers on Amazon Prime*, they can upgrade their shipping options in order to eligible FBA listings.

* This excludes multi-channel fulfillment orders that have been placed on other websites and services that include Amazon Webstore or the Checkout by Amazon.

STEP #4: Amazon Will Be The Ones To Pick And Pack Your Products

The products for sale that have been ordered by customers will be picked and packaged for delivery

This is how it works:
- Amazon will be the one to locate your products through the use of advanced web-to-warehouse, high-speed picking and a sorting system that Amazon has developed

- Customers are allowed to combine different ordered with other products that have been fulfilled by Amazon

STEP #5: Amazon Then Ships Your Products To The Customers

Amazon will then be able to ship the products the customers have requested through their network of fulfillment centers

This is how it works:
- Amazon will choose whichever method is comfortable for them for shipping

- Tracking information is provided for the customers

- For orders placed on Amazon.com, customers are able to contact customer's services for any inquiries.

YouTube Video Tutorials
- **How Fulfillment by Amazon (FBA) works:** https://goo.gl/cRWhEE
- **Tour of Fulfillment by Amazon (FBA):** https://goo.gl/1D6usZ
- **How Amazon Receives Your Inventory:** https://goo.gl/CAAYgH

- **Amazon FBA - What It Is And How it Works!:** https://goo.gl/smjfN8
- **How to Start an Online Business on Amazon the RIGHT way with no Technical Knowledge:** https://goo.gl/R8xBZu

c. Why Is FBA a Big Deal?

With all the big buzz of Fulfillment by Amazon, some sellers may be wondering: FBA is just another fulfillment method, isn't it? What's all this talk about the use of FBA? Basically, **What's the big deal about FBA**?

FBA becomes a big deal once you realize the amount of support it can place on your online business. For some, it becomes a **major decision** in their business in terms of profit that they will be making during their online career.

Those who may get to feel the best effect of the FBA are those who are small business owners, these people may not have the most efficient fulfillment systems in their arsenal and may not want to risk any potential negative effects from a poor customer experience.

Although there is plenty amounts of benefits that a seller can gain from using FBA, you should also never forget the following:

- Not every third-party seller should use FBA; it all really depends on the individual seller's financial resources as well as the nature of his or her business.

- Sellers should look at FBA as another weapon in their arsenal and not as a blanket resource. Sellers should either be 100% FBA or 100% FBM (Fulfillment by Merchant), although most professional sellers have become a hybrid of both

- Not all the products that have been submitted for FBA will end up being a good candidate for a number of reasons, mainly size, performance of their sales and their margin.

d. How FBA affects Product Discoverability and Buyability?

Before we get into learning on how FBA affects product Discoverability and Buyability, we will first look into the two terms:

1. Discoverability
This is the ability for your product listing to be found on Amazon. Amazon focuses on the type of search results on the different products rather than the type of seller

When it comes to having people be able to reach your products, FBA products are indeed the ones who get more discoverable for two reasons:

Reason #1: Amazon Prime Members

Prime members are those who spend more time shopping on Amazon than the average customer. These customers are entitled to filtering out all the non-Prime offers, which basically takes away those products that aren't in the FBA listing system.

Reason #2: Amazon's Reputation

Even if your product does by chance show up on the shoppers list, there will be items that will possess the offer that shows *'Fulfillment by Amazon'* and are more desirable for customers due to the efficient and traceable delivery process

2. Buyability

A product's likelihood of being bought or in more actionable terms, this is the product's chance of winning the Buy Box

Here are the effects on Buyability:

Reason #1: Seller's Rating

FBA sellers will not gain any negative ratings on the metrics of On-Time Delivery Rate and Late Shipment Rate due to FBA.

Reason #2: Fulfillment Latency

FBA items are instantly placed in the shortest latency windows, while FBM offers might proceed to be in longer windows (ex. 3-4 business days)

e. Advantages of Amazon FBA

Using Fulfillment by Amazon offers huge benefits for sellers like you. Here are the best benefits you can get by using Amazon FBA:

1- Accessibility to the Prime Members

As an online seller, you couldn't ask for a better customer. These Prime Members subscribe at least $99 a year in order to take full advantage of the free shipping that Amazon has to offer.

These Prime Members are not only loyal customers, but they are the ones who tend to purchase items that are more expensive and buy at least %150 more than any of the non-Prime Members. To see these in number basis, they spend around $1,340 on Amazon annually, while non-Prime Members spend only around %529

The use of FBA allows for a wider customer base. There is a speculation of around 50 million Prime Member subscribers in Amazon right now. If you think about, that's a lot of money.

2 - The Care for Shipping, Returns, and Customer Service

Amazon handles everything from picking the item, packing it and shipping it to your customers. Quick and swift shipping gives you happy customers and with happy customers provides with increased sales.

Amazon will also be able to handle any of the unsatisfied customers. This will definitely save the time and money for you because you won't need to employ any additional customer service reps.

Since your items will be stored in Amazon's fulfillment centers, you won't need to gain the headache of where to get the space to fit your inventory.

3 - Buy Box Win

Those in FBA, depending on the category of the product, can place its price at least 10 – 20% higher than the average competitor and still be able to win the Buy Box. That is if you are using FBA and your competitors are not.

This is because shipping is added into the cost. If your items are priced at $20 with a Prime Member shipping, it will beat out a merchant item of $15 with $5 shipping.

4 - Increased Volume of Sales

This may not be a guarantee, but it has been found that those who switch over recognize a rise in unit sales volume to about 20% more. Numerous amounts of sellers have reported higher or even double of their original volume. This is mainly due to the Prime Member subscribers.

5 - Customers are Inclined to Pay More for the Same Product

The millions of Prime Member subscribers on Amazon will know a great deal when they see it. As mentioned in one of the benefits, sellers who are in FBA could factor in the cost of shipping into the price. Some Prime Members are willing to pay a few more bucks to be able to ensure that the delivery is prompted in two days and the added convenience.

6 - No Such Thing as an Inventory Limit

Since Amazon does your inventory for you, you can sell as much as you want without the worry of the amount of storage requirements that you need. Amazon possesses one of the most advanced fulfillment networks in the whole world that will allow you, as a seller, to store as much products as you please with the use of their automated inventory tracker. Your products are guaranteed safety.

YouTube Video Tutorials
- **Amazon FBA: 3 Benefits to Selling on Amazon FBA:** https://goo.gl/LqpiWG
- **Pros and Cons of Selling on Amazon:** https://goo.gl/ecmWV9
- **Amazon FBA Canada: Pros & Cons of FBA** Canada: **https://goo.gl/n5SFra**

f. Disadvantages of Amazon FBA

Like any other business, Amazon FBA also comes with some disadvantages that a seller has to deal with. Here are some Amazon FBA disadvantages you should take in mind:

1 - Not All Products Sold are Profitable with FBA

The products that have a low volume and low margins are the ones that will end up not being profitable to sell with the use of FBA. Furthermore, any items that are heavy and inexpensive low margin items that may require for you to have higher storage fees may be the items that blow out your profits.

2 - Amazon Will Not Be Able to Ship Certain Items

Some items that may be deemed as hazardous are severely prohibited and these items will not be shipped by the Amazon's fulfillment centers. Examples of these items include: any type of flammable liquids, flammable solids, and aerosols. Some beauty products may fall under this category.

3 - Fees, Glorious Fees

FBA may seem like a miracle service, although there are some pitfalls with its use. The biggest one among many of its pitfalls is the numerous amounts of fees associated with FBA.

To start, sellers on Amazon are required to either have a Pro Merchant ($39.95/month) account or the Advantage account ($29.95/year), which have different limitations to what a seller can and cannot do.

Next, FBA charges a certain amount for storage fee for the items that are unsold in Amazon's fulfillment centers. When your items don't sell, FBA customers are charged at rates that can vary from $0.40/cubic foot per month to $0.60 cubic foot per month.

Overall, depending on the type of online business that you are in, you might want to proceed with FBA or not. Take your time to think about it because if it is good for your business it can go far, although if it is not it may destroy what you built.

YouTube Video Tutorials

- Part 1: **What Is FBA? - The Introduction:**
  https://goo.gl/rJCghN
- Part 2: **Signing up for FBA & Sourcing:**
  https://goo.gl/dFPMmc
- Part 3: **Organizing and Listing Inventory:**
  https://goo.gl/VSEpVH
- Part 4: **Rules, Guidelines, and Supplies:**
  https://goo.gl/QnvW9v
- Part 5: **Packaging Your First Shipment:**
  https://goo.gl/Wh2uCW, **How to Package Items
  For Amazon FBA - Save Money & Clear Up
  Misconceptions:** https://goo.gl/QyZGG6
- Part 6: **Finalizing Your First Shipment:**
  https://goo.gl/e6ypDK
- All Parts: **The Complete Series:**
  https://goo.gl/vp8sK2

To get this more advanced book on Amazon FBA, fully packed with highly valuable information, just click the link below to open the Amazon Kindle book page.

Get this book:

View in Amazon Kindle Store: http://goo.gl/6flafa

Free Resources:

Facebook Page:
www.facebook.com/surefiresuccessnow

Website: www.workathomeentrepreneurblog.com